U.S. LANDMARKS

STATUE OF LIBERTY

Amy Culliford

TABLE OF CONTENTS

A Pelican Book
SEAHORSE PUBLISHING

Teaching Tips for Caregivers and Teachers:

Research shows that one of the best ways for students to learn a new topic is to read about it.

Before Reading

- Read the title and predict what the book will be about.
- Read the "Words to Know" and discuss the meaning of each word.
- Read the back cover to see what the book is about.

During Reading

- When a student gets to a word that is unknown, ask them to look at the rest of the sentence to find clues to help with the meaning of the unknown word.
- Motivate students with praise and encouragement.

After Reading

- Discuss the main idea of the book.
- Ask students to give one detail that they learned in the book.

Sight Words

a	in	people
at	is	see
can	it	tall
day	made	that
every	many	the
go	night	to
has	of	you
I	out	

Words to Know

copper

New York

sculpture

Statue of Liberty

torch

Statue of Liberty

I see the **Statue of Liberty**!

The Statue of Liberty is in **New York**.

UNITED STATES OF AMERICA

It is a tall **sculpture**.

sculpture

It is made out of **copper**.

copper

It has a **torch** that you can see at night.

torch

Many people go to see the Statue of Liberty every day!

Index

Written by: Amy Culliford
Design by: Under the Oaks Media
Series Development: James Earley
Editor: Kim Thompson

Photos: Thongchais: cover; Leon Bijelic: p. 4-5; Victor Maschek: p. 9; luca amedi: p. 11; Cincila; p. 12-13; Matej Hudovernik: p. 15

Library of Congress PCN Data
Statue of Liberty / Amy Culliford
U.S. Landmarks
ISBN 978-1-63897-076-7 (hard cover)
ISBN 978-1-63897-162-7 (paperback)
ISBN 978-1-63897-248-8 (EPUB)
ISBN 978-1-63897-334-8 (eBook)
Library of Congress Control Number: 2021945247

Printed in the United States of America.

Seahorse Publishing Company
www.seahorsepub.com

Published in the United States
Seahorse Publishing
PO Box 771325
Coral Springs, FL 33077

SEAHORSE PUBLISHING